Lerner SPORTS™

SPORTS ALL-STARS

CARSON WENTZ

Anthony K. Hewson

Lerner Publications ◆ Minneapolis

Lerner Publications Company
A division of Lerner Publishing Group, Inc.
241 First Avenue North
Minneapolis, MN 55401 USA

For reading levels and more information, look up this title at www.lernerbooks.com.

Main body text set in Albany Std.
Typeface provided by Agfa.

Library of Congress Cataloging-in-Publication Data
Names: Hewson, Anthony K., author.
Title: Carson Wentz / by Anthony K. Hewson.
Description: Minneapolis : Lerner Publications, [2020] | Series: Sports All-Stars | Audience: Ages: 7–11. | Audience: Grades: 4 to 6. | Includes webography. | Includes bibliographical references and index.
Identifiers: LCCN 2019002742 (print) | LCCN 2019004537 (ebook) | ISBN 9781541556225 (eb pdf) | ISBN 9781541556126 (library binding : alk. paper) | ISBN 9781541574489 (paperback : alk. paper)
Subjects: LCSH: Wentz, Carson, 1992-—Juvenile literature. | Quarterbacks (Football)—United States—Juvenile literature. | Football players—United States—Biography—Juvenile literature. | North Dakota State University—Football—History—Juvenile literature. | Philadelphia Eagles (Football team)—History—Juvenile literature.
Classification: LCC GV939.W46 (ebook) | LCC GV939.W46 H48 2019 (print) | DDC 796.332092—dc23

LC record available at https://lccn.loc.gov/2019002742

Manufactured in the United States of America
1-CG-7/15/19

CONTENTS

PUTTING PHILLY IN THE PLAYOFFS

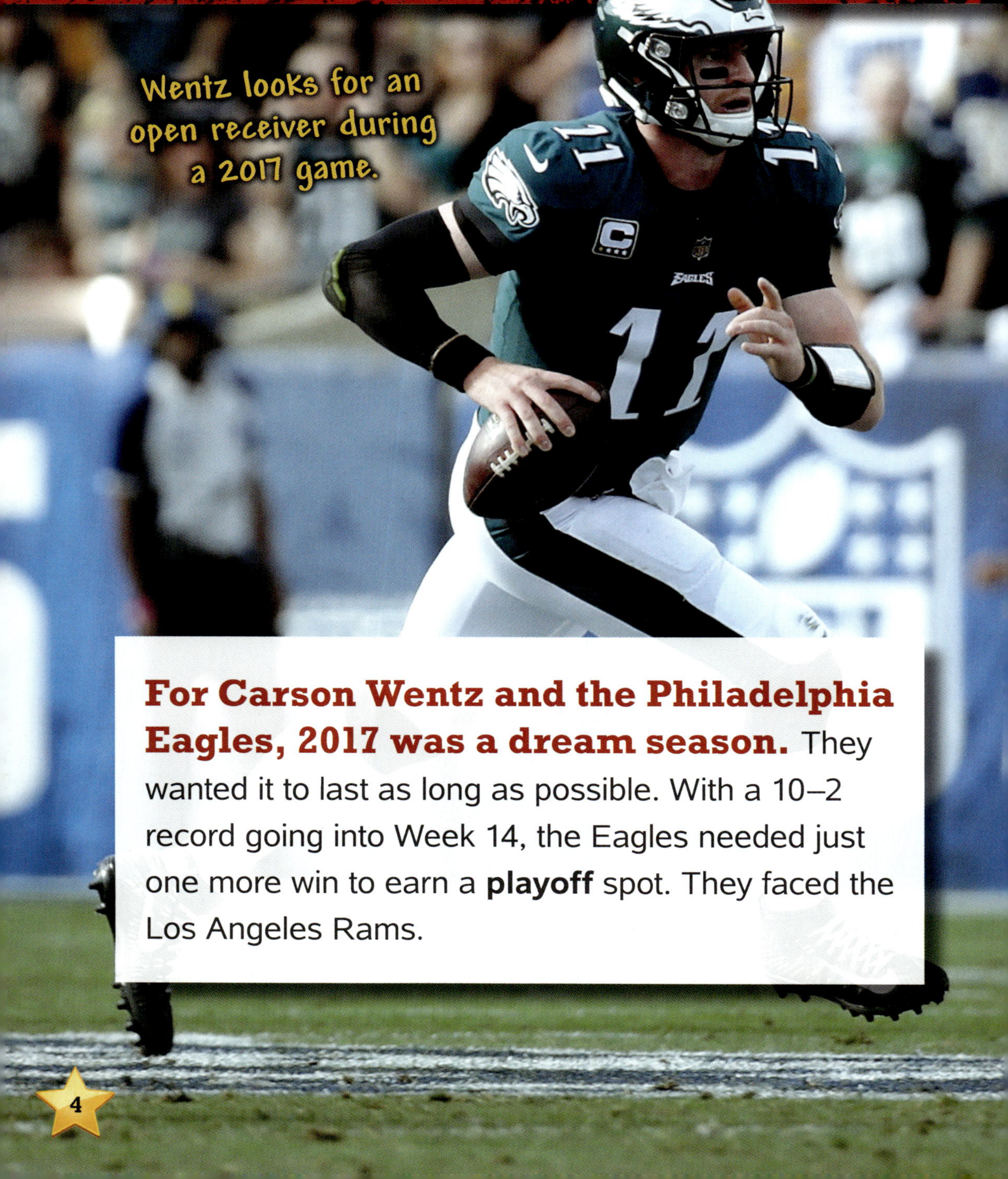

Wentz looks for an open receiver during a 2017 game.

For Carson Wentz and the Philadelphia Eagles, 2017 was a dream season. They wanted it to last as long as possible. With a 10–2 record going into Week 14, the Eagles needed just one more win to earn a **playoff** spot. They faced the Los Angeles Rams.

FACTS AT A GLANCE

- **Date of Birth:** December 30, 1992
- **Position:** quarterback
- **League:** National Football League (NFL)
- **Professional Highlights:** drafted second overall by the Philadelphia Eagles in 2016; started all 16 games in his **rookie** season; set an NFL record for most pass completions by a rookie; had an 11–2 record in 2017 as the Eagles won Super Bowl LII
- **Personal Highlights:** started the AO1 Foundation in 2017; enjoys hunting in his home state, North Dakota; got married in 2018

Wentz throws the ball as Los Angeles Rams players move in on him.

Wentz had put together a great season. It was just his second year in the NFL. But he was playing like a Most Valuable Player (MVP). He threw for 3,296 yards with 33 touchdowns that season.

Wentz played great against the Rams. In the first half alone, he threw three touchdown passes. The Eagles had a 24–14 lead at halftime. But their season turned upside down in the third quarter. As Wentz was running toward the end zone, two Rams players hit him. Wentz was slow to get up but stayed in the game.

Wentz threw another touchdown pass three plays later. But he could not put any weight on his left leg. He was too hurt to keep playing. The Eagles went on to win the game and make the playoffs. But Wentz had a serious knee injury.

Wentz had to miss the rest of the season. But he cheered for his teammates and offered whatever help he could. He was thrilled to watch them win the Super Bowl. But next time, Wentz wanted to be on the field himself.

Wentz dives across the goal line in a game against the Los Angeles Rams.

NORTH DAKOTA KID

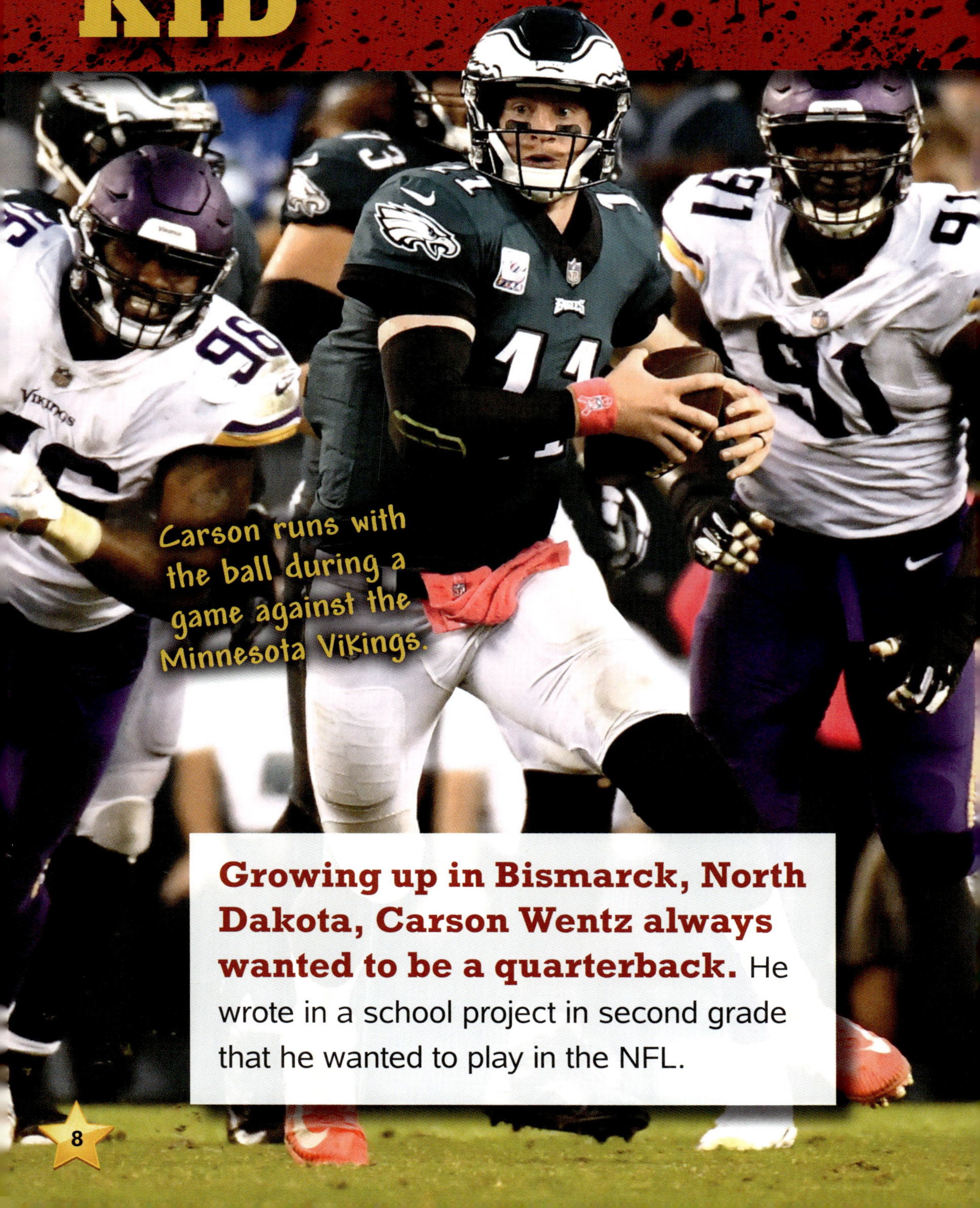

Carson runs with the ball during a game against the Minnesota Vikings.

Growing up in Bismarck, North Dakota, Carson Wentz always wanted to be a quarterback. He wrote in a school project in second grade that he wanted to play in the NFL.

Carson was born on December 30, 1992, and grew up watching the Minnesota Vikings. He liked watching the games on TV, but he loved playing catch with his dad at halftime even more. Sometimes they would miss the second half of the game because Carson wanted to keep playing.

Carson went to Century High School in Bismarck.

When he entered high school, Carson still dreamed of being a star quarterback. The only problem was he was 5 feet 8 inches (1.73 m) tall and weighed about 125 pounds (57 kg). He used to pray that he would grow to be 6 feet (1.83 m) tall.

By his senior year of high school, Carson had grown to 6 feet 5 inches (1.96 m) and weighed 200 pounds (91 kg). He became the starting quarterback on his high school team. He threw 25 touchdown passes that year. He was one of the best players in the state.

But there weren't many colleges **recruiting** Carson to play football. He had just one year as a starting quarterback. And his home state of North Dakota was not known for producing top college players.

Carson played quarterback for his college team.

Carson accepted a **scholarship** from North Dakota State University (NDSU). The school had a great football program. The Bison were one of the best teams in the Football Championship **Subdivision** (FCS), the second-highest level of college football.

The Bison won the national championship all four years Carson attended. Carson was named starting quarterback his junior year. NDSU went 15–1 that year, and Carson threw for 3,111 yards and 25 touchdowns. He also ran for 642 yards and scored six touchdowns.

Carson became a star for the NDSU Bison.

Carson was on track to do even better during his senior year. He missed eight games with a broken wrist. But he still threw for 1,651 yards and 17 touchdowns that year. He played in the national championship game, where he led the Bison to victory.

Not many FCS players get drafted in the NFL. Even fewer are quarterbacks. But teams saw something special with Carson. He had the size and strong arm it takes to be an NFL quarterback. He showed he was a hard worker at NDSU.

That was enough for the Philadelphia Eagles to choose Carson as the second overall pick in the 2016 NFL Draft. He was the highest draft pick ever chosen from an FCS school.

"He's a winner," Eagles coach Doug Pederson said after the draft.

Carson just had to go out and prove it.

Carson was one of just two FCS quarterbacks starting for an NFL team in 2016. The other was Joe Flacco of the Baltimore Ravens. He attended the University of Delaware.

Carson holds up an Eagles jersey after being drafted.

A CLASSIC QUARTERBACK

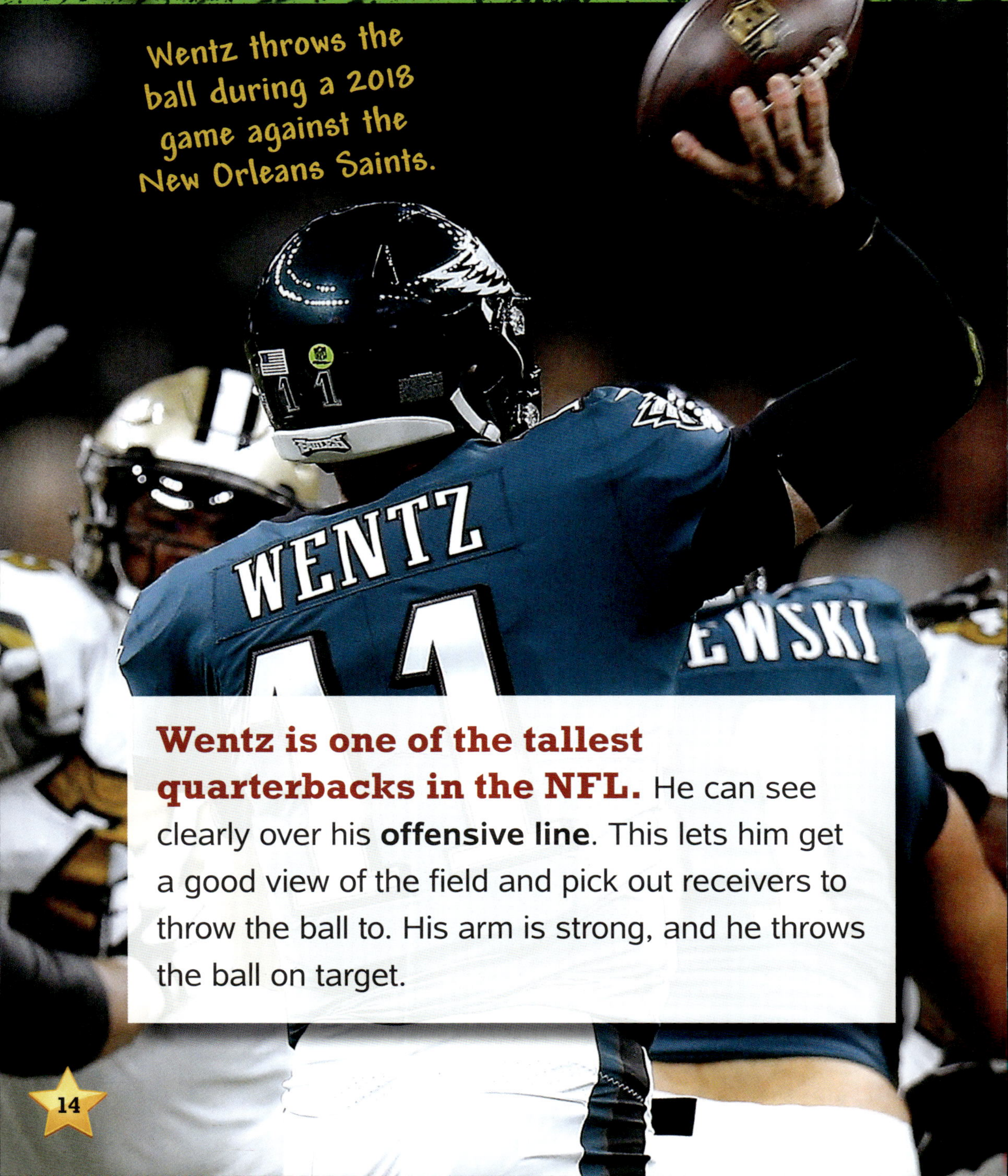

Wentz throws the ball during a 2018 game against the New Orleans Saints.

Wentz is one of the tallest quarterbacks in the NFL. He can see clearly over his **offensive line**. This lets him get a good view of the field and pick out receivers to throw the ball to. His arm is strong, and he throws the ball on target.

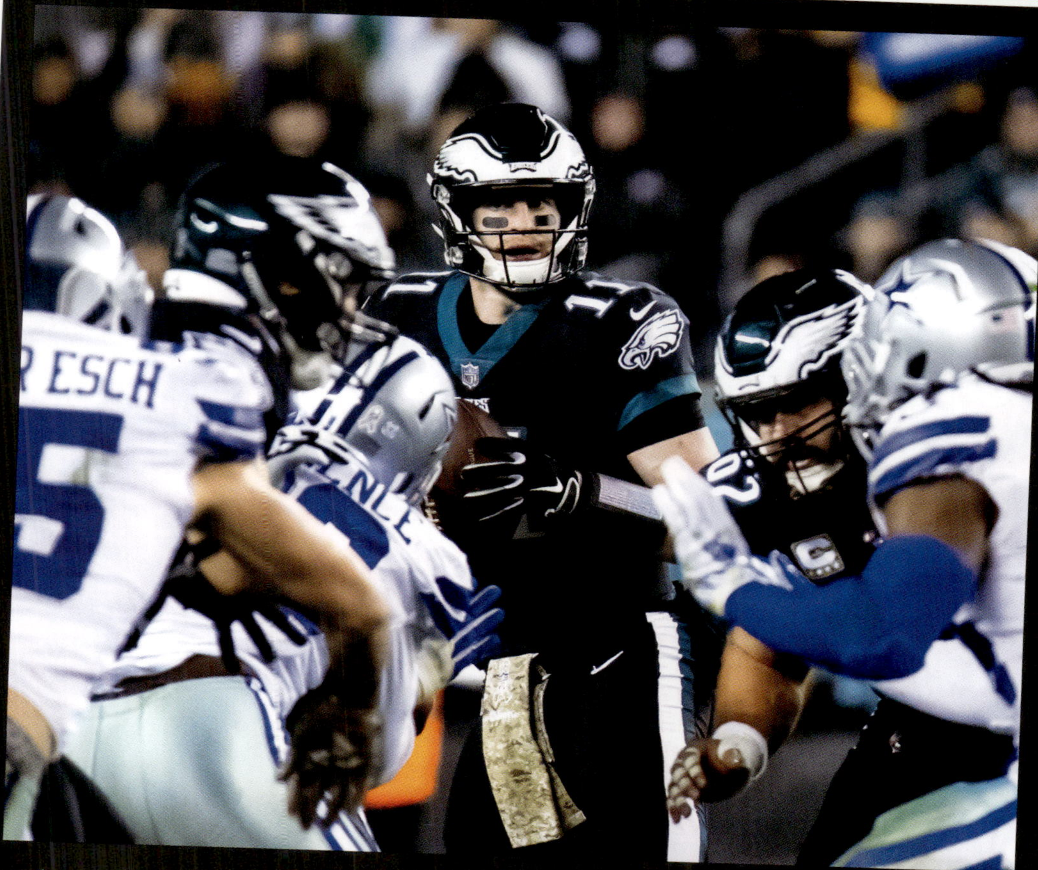

Wentz looks for receivers in a game against the Dallas Cowboys.

Wentz makes sure his body is ready to compete. During football season, he does strength training and practices plays with his teammates.

Wentz works hard in the **off-season** to stay in shape. He likes to swim because swimming is not as hard on the body as some other workouts.

Only a few quarterbacks in the NFL are taller than Wentz. Two of them also played for the Eagles in 2018. Nick Foles and Nate Sudfeld are both one inch (2.5 cm) taller than Wentz.

But it still gives him the exercise he needs to stay healthy. Wentz does not try to swim as fast as possible. He just tries to get a good workout.

What Wentz does before and after working out is also important. Wentz stretches because it helps warm up the body and reduces the risk of injury. Even a pulled muscle can put an athlete out of the game.

During the 2018 off-season, Wentz had to recover from his knee injury before he could work out normally. He did exercises to improve his knee's flexibility and strength. He also worked out with other injured Eagles players. Together, they made their way back to full health.

Wentz was ready to play by Week 3 of the 2018 season thanks to his off-season workouts.

WENTZ OFF THE FIELD

Wentz wears an A01 Foundation shirt during practice.

Football is just one of Wentz's interests.
He loves spending time outdoors and helping others. In 2017 he started an organization that combines those interests.

Wentz's AO1 tattoo is visible as he warms up before a game.

Wentz started his own **charity** called the AO1 Foundation. AO1 stands for "audience of one." That phrase has strong meaning for Wentz. It reminds him that everything he does in his life is connected to his Christian beliefs. Wentz has an AO1 tattoo on his right wrist.

Wentz started the AO1 Foundation to help improve the lives of people in need. The organization helps people in Philadelphia and around the world.

AO1 workers drive a food truck around Philadelphia and give free food to hungry people. Wentz himself sometimes works on the truck.

AO1 began building a sports complex for kids in Haiti in 2017. Haiti is a poor country. Many kids there can't go to big sports fields or gyms to play sports. AO1's sports complex will give thousands of kids that opportunity.

Many kids in Haiti can't play sports at large gyms or sports fields.

Wentz sometimes features AO1 on his shoes during games.

Wentz and some of his Eagles teammates have spent time in Haiti during the off-season to help build the complex.

Back in the United States, Wentz shares his love of the outdoors through AO1's outdoor program. AO1 operates a camp where kids play outdoors, learn skills, ride horses, and just have fun.

Wentz brought his mom to an event that celebrated the NFL Draft after he was selected by the Eagles.

Wentz loves his family and his home state. When he is back in North Dakota, Wentz loves hunting and fishing. He even hosts his own TV show with his brother. It shows them on hunting and fishing adventures.

On February 4, 2018, Wentz got a ring for the Eagles' Super Bowl win. Two days later, he gave his girlfriend a ring and asked her to marry him. Wentz and Madison Oberg were married in July of that year.

Major League Baseball player Mike Trout
watches an Eagles game.

LEADING THE EAGLES

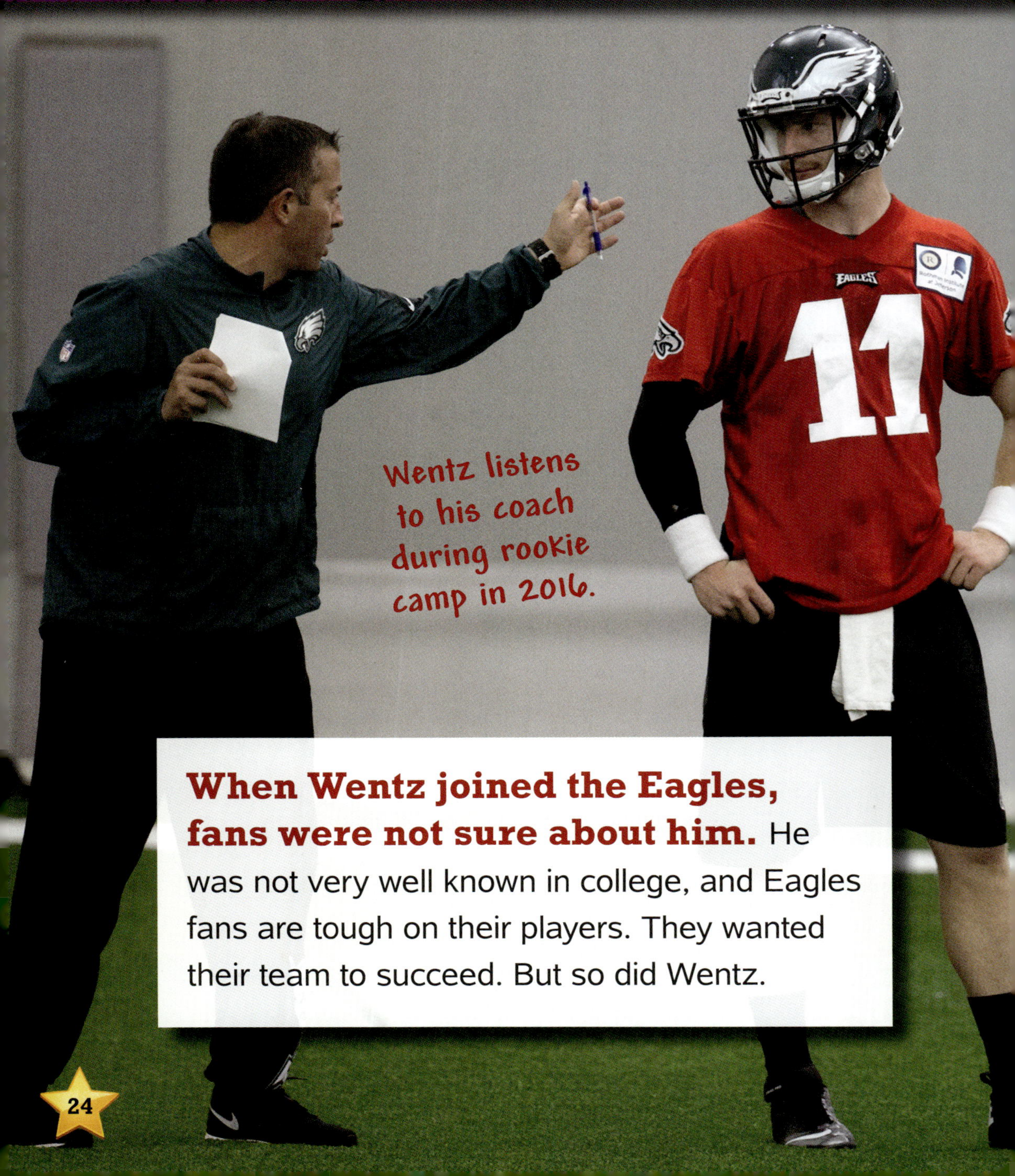

Wentz listens to his coach during rookie camp in 2016.

When Wentz joined the Eagles, fans were not sure about him. He was not very well known in college, and Eagles fans are tough on their players. They wanted their team to succeed. But so did Wentz.

“They’re **passionate** here,” Wentz said. “I’m like, ‘Heck, I fit right in.’”

Wentz started off well. He threw five touchdown passes and no **interceptions** in his first three games. On November 13, 2016, he led a game-winning **drive** against the Atlanta Falcons. But overall, Wentz did not have a great rookie season. He threw 16 touchdown passes, but he also threw 14 interceptions.

Wentz fights for extra yards against the Arizona Cardinals.

The Eagles needed Wentz to make big progress. He reduced his interception rate in 2017. He also improved his **accuracy** on deep throws. In Week 5 against the Arizona Cardinals, Wentz threw touchdown passes of 59 and 72 yards.

Wentz stands with teammate Nick Foles on the sidelines.

Wentz was getting a lot of attention for how well he was playing. It looked like he might win the MVP award that year. Then he got hurt. His chance at MVP was gone. But he stuck with his team.

"Carson's there every day, and that's important," said teammate Malcolm Jenkins.

Wentz was on the sidelines helping his backup, Nick Foles. He went to practice and helped the coaches prepare. Everyone's hard work paid off. The Eagles went 13–3 and made it all the way to the Super Bowl. They beat the New England Patriots for their first Super Bowl championship.

Wentz did not want to miss another run at a title. He worked hard in the off-season to come back from his injury. He was not ready for the start of the 2018 season. But he came back in Week 3. Wentz looked like his old self. He even showed he was not afraid to dive. Needing a first down, Wentz ran with the ball and dived forward to make the play.

In 2018 the Eagles struggled to regain their Super Bowl form. But Wentz had even better numbers than in 2017. The Eagles knew that at least they could count on him.

Wentz looks for a receiver during a 2018 game.

After watching his team win a Super Bowl, Wentz was focused on winning one on the field. But an injury in December 2018 kept him out of the playoffs again. He supported his teammates, but they lost to the New Orleans Saints in the second round. Wentz worked toward getting healthy again so he could be ready for the next season and another chance at the Super Bowl.

All-Star Stats

Wentz has quickly become one of the best quarterbacks in Eagles history. His career numbers are impressive. Passer rating is a way to measure how well a quarterback is playing. Here is where Wentz ranked through 2018 among quarterbacks who have thrown at least 100 passes for the Eagles:

Eagles Quarterbacks Passer Ratings through 2018

1. Jeff Garcia, 95.8
2. Nick Foles, 93.2
3. Carson Wentz, 92.5
4. Michael Vick, 87.7
5. Mark Sanchez, 86.6
6. Donovan McNabb, 86.5
7. Sam Bradford, 86.4
8. Bubby Brister, 85.8
9. Sonny Jurgensen, 79.1
10. Randall Cunningham, 78.7

Source Notes

12. Phil Sheridan, "Eagles Pick Quarterback Carson Wentz in First Round," *ESPN.com*, April 28, 2016, http://www.espn.com/blog/philadelphia-eagles/post/_/id/16719/eagles-pick-qb-carson-wentz-in-first-round

25. "Quotes on Carson Wentz," *PhiladelphiaEagles.com*, https://www.philadelphiaeagles.com/photos/quotes-on-carson-wentz-17100866#dfffbf3c-aa18-47f3-8916-885d47c49577

26. Tim McManus, "Why the Eagles Are Playing for Jason Peters, Carson Wentz," *ESPN.com*, January 22, 2018, http://www.espn.com/blog/philadelphia-eagles/post/_/id/24083/eagles-playing-for-teammates-who-cant

Glossary

accuracy: being on target in doing something

charity: an organization that helps other people or raises money for a good cause

drive: a series of plays that move the ball down the field toward the opponent's end zone

interceptions: catches made by a defensive player when the ball was meant for an offensive player

offensive line: football players who block for the quarterback and running backs

off-season: the time of year when a sports league is not playing

passionate: believing very strongly in something

playoff: a game after the regular season that determines which teams will compete for the championship

recruiting: when a college team tries to get a high school athlete to compete for them

rookie: an athlete who is in his first season with a sports team

scholarship: money given to someone to go to college

subdivision: a smaller part of a larger group

Further Information

Carson Wentz Career Stats
https://www.pro-football-reference.com/players/W/WentCa00.htm

Carson Wentz College Stats
https://www.sports-reference.com/cfb/players/carson-wentz-1.html

Carson Wentz Philadelphia Eagles Bio
https://www.philadelphiaeagles.com/team/players-roster/carson-wentz/

Mack, Larry. *The Philadelphia Eagles Story*. Minneapolis: Bellwether Media, 2017.

Savage, Jeff. *Football Super Stats*. Minneapolis: Lerner Publications, 2018.

Scheff, Matt. *Carson Wentz: Football Star*. Lake Elmo, MN: Focus Readers, 2019.

Index

Photo Acknowledgments

The images in this book are used with the permission of: © Jeff Gross/Getty Images Sport/Getty Images, pp. 4-5, 7; © Chris Williams/Icon Sportswire/Getty Images, p. 6; © Andy Lewis/Icon Sportswire/Getty Images, p. 8; © Seth Poppel/Yearbook Library, p. 9; © Matthew Pearce/Icon Sportswire/Corbis/Getty Images, p. 10; © Steve Nurenberg/Icon Sportswire/Corbis/Getty Images, p. 11; © Jon Durr/Getty Images Sport/Getty Images, p. 13; © Jonathan Bachman/Getty Images Sport/Getty Images, p. 14; © Brett Carlsen/Getty Images Sport/Getty Images, pp. 15, 18, 23, 26; © Nick Cammett/Diamond Images/Getty Images, p. 17; © Mitchell Leff/Getty Images Sport/Getty Images, pp. 19, 21, 24; © arindambanerjee/Shutterstock.com, p. 20; © Kena Krutsinger/Getty Images Sport/Getty Images, p. 22; © Rich Schultz/Getty Images Sport/Getty Images, p. 25; © Ronald C. Modra/Sports Imagery/Getty Images Sport/Getty Images, p. 27.

Front Cover: © Chris Williams/Icon Sportswire/Getty Images.